50 Quick and Brilliant Teaching Techniques

By Mike Gershon

Text Copyright © 2014 Mike Gershon

All Rights Reserved

About the Author

Mike Gershon is a teacher, trainer and writer. He is the author of twenty books on teaching, learning and education, including a number of bestsellers, as well as the co-author of one other. Mike's online resources have been viewed and downloaded more than 2.5 million times by teachers in over 180 countries and territories. He is a regular contributor to the Times Educational Supplement and has created a series of electronic CPD guides for TES PRO. Find out more, get in touch and download free resources at www.mikegershon.com

Training and Consultancy

Mike is an expert trainer whose sessions have received acclaim from teachers across England. Recent bookings include:

- *Improving Literacy Levels in Every Classroom*, St Leonard's Academy, Sussex

- *Growth Mindsets, Effective Marking and Feedback* Ash Manor School, Aldershot

- *Effective Differentiation,* Tri-Borough Alternative Provision (TBAP), London

Mike also works as a consultant, advising on teaching and learning and creating bespoke materials for schools. Recent work includes:

- *Developing and Facilitating Independent Learning,* Chipping Norton School, Oxfordshire

- *Differentiation In-Service Training,* Charles Darwin School, Kent

If you would like speak to Mike about the services he can offer your school, please get in touch by email: mike@mikegershon.com

Other Works from the Same Authors

Available to buy now on Amazon:

How to use Differentiation in the Classroom: The Complete Guide

How to use Assessment for Learning in the Classroom: The Complete Guide

How to use Questioning in the Classroom: The Complete Guide

How to use Discussion in the Classroom: The Complete Guide

How to Teach EAL Students in the Classroom: The Complete Guide

More Secondary Starters and Plenaries

Secondary Starters and Plenaries: History

Teach Now! History: Becoming a Great History Teacher

The Growth Mindset Pocketbook (with Professor Barry Hymer)

How to be Outstanding in the Classroom

Also available to buy now on Amazon, the entire 'Quick 50' Series:

50 Quick and Brilliant Teaching Ideas

50 Quick and Brilliant Teaching Techniques

50 Quick and Easy Lesson Activities

50 Quick Ways to Help Your Students Secure A and B Grades at GCSE

50 Quick Ways to Help Your Students Think, Learn, and Use Their Brains Brilliantly

50 Quick Ways to Motivate and Engage Your Students

50 Quick Ways to Outstanding Teaching

50 Quick Ways to Perfect Behaviour Management

50 Quick and Brilliant Teaching Games

50 Quick and Easy Ways to Outstanding Group Work

50 Quick and Easy Ways to Prepare for Ofsted

50 Quick and Easy Ways Leaders can Prepare for Ofsted

About the Series

The 'Quick 50' series was born out of a desire to provide teachers with practical, tried and tested ideas, activities, strategies and techniques which would help them to teach brilliant lessons, raise achievement and engage and inspire their students.

Every title in the series distils great teaching wisdom into fifty bite-sized chunks. These are easy to digest and easy to apply – perfect for the busy teacher who wants to develop their practice and support their students.

Acknowledgements

As ever I must thank all the fantastic colleagues and students I have worked with over the years, first while training at the Institute of Education, Central Foundation Girls' School and Nower Hill High School and subsequently while working at Pimlico Academy and King Edward VI School in Bury St Edmunds.

Thanks also to Alison and Andrew Metcalfe for a great place to write and finally to Gordon at KallKwik for help with the covers.

Table of Contents

Introduction

Praise Hunt

Pupils set the Homework

Scrap Paper

New Rules

Clean Slate

Fall-Back Lessons

Plan for Errors

Prompt Cards

Accept No Guessing

No Hands Up

Answer Tokens

Joker Cards

Work the Room

Break it Down

Activity Stations

Hand Gestures

Scanning

Only Share Times If They Are Definite

Speak As You Mean To Go On

Sit Back and Let Go

Fast, Slow, Fast, Slow

Mini-Plenaries

Get Connected

Have Everything Ready

Vary Your Pitch

Tempo

Mirroring

Build Rapport

Name Recognition

Success Criteria

Task List

Checklists

Sightlines

Process Training

Start of Year Certificates

Speaking and Listening Rules

Always Start With an Example

Wait-Time

Entry Slips

Scribe

Starting Routines

Ending Routines

Manage Transitions

Repetition

Play Dumb

Play Smart

Play Helpful

Play Random

Postcards

The Evaluation Tree

A Brief Request

Introduction

Welcome to '50 Quick and Brilliant Teaching Techniques.'

This book is all about the things you can do inside and outside the classroom to make great learning happen, to create engaging, inspiring lessons and to get the very best out of the students you teach.

All the entries in the book are practical and easy to implement. They stem from my own experience as a teacher and trainer. You can use them across the curriculum and with different age groups.

No entry is set in stone. You should feel free to adapt and develop the techniques so they suit your teaching style and meet the needs of the pupils you teach.

So read on and be inspired – every entry is waiting to provide you with a fantastic way in which to raise standards, teach brilliant lessons and make great learning happen!

Praise Hunt

01 Let's start with praise. Everyone works better when they feel appreciated. Everyone likes to know that someone else thinks they're doing a good job. Everyone values praise highly when it is genuine, specific and given for a good reason.

Sometimes we don't think there are many opportunities to praise students. But there are. You just have to hunt them out.

When your pupils are working, walk around the room and see what they are doing; listen to them; read their work. Find things to praise them for, genuinely and precisely. Go on a praise hunt every lesson. Your students will respond; motivation will rise and, so too, will the atmosphere in the room.

Pupils set the Homework

02 Ah, homework. The last frontier of school, wherein the exigencies of the classroom reach out into the world of home, calling insistently to be met by pupils, one and all.

Instead of setting the homework yourself, you can invite your students to set it. Doing this completely changes the idea of what homework is. It stops being an imposition by the teacher and starts being a negotiation.

You might let pupils decide the homework in full, or you might provide them with a range of choices from which to select. Either way, motivation, engagement and a sense of ownership will develop as a result.

Scrap Paper

03 We have limitations. I know, I know, we don't like to admit it, but it's true. Despite my best efforts I know that I am not going to be a professional footballer. Nor will I ever build up enough spring in my step to leap over tall buildings.

Similarly, all of us live daily with the fact that our short-term memory is limited. Psychologists say the range is about 7 separate pieces of information, plus or minus two.

This can get in the way of things.

That's why we use tools to expand our memory – reference works, reminders, shopping lists.

A great tool to get students using in the classroom is scrap paper. This can act as an expansion of their short-term memory because it provides space in which to write things down, try things out and park ideas. Have some to hand in your classroom and encourage its use.

New Rules

04 Midway through an activity, student interest may start to sag. Active thinking may begin to slide towards the realms of passivity.

This is not what we want. It will limit progress and slow the pace of learning.

If you come across such a situation, counter it by changing the rules of the activity half way through. You could throw in something new that pupils need to do. Or you could introduce a new idea or piece of information for them to analyse. Or, you could bring up a completely different perspective and ask students to think about how this changes everything they have so far been thinking about.

New rules help ensure motivation, focus and application remain high throughout the duration of a task.

Clean Slate

05 This is such a simple technique. Not only does it work brilliantly but its effects are often both significant and clearly visible.

Every time you start a new lesson, do so with a clean slate. Forget about what the pupils did last lesson (well, not what they learnt about obviously!) and see them afresh.

Approaching your teaching in this way avoids labelling, acknowledges the fact that young people are learning all the time and often make mistakes, and also gives every pupil who crosses your path the opportunity to be whoever they want to be each time they come into your classroom.

Remember, some students might spend their whole school career being labelled. Then they come into your room and see that you treat them differently. You give them a clean slate. What an effect that can have!

Fall-Back Lessons

06 Let's face it. Sometimes it all goes wrong. Whether it's you, the students, the technology, the weather, the noise from next door or something else, these things happen.

By having a fall-back lesson ready you can minimise any disruption which might develop should one of these situations arise.

Fall-back lessons are those you can pull out at any time to use with any class when teaching any topic. It might be a particular lesson you know always works well. Or it might be a lesson which involves quiet, independent work (thus reigning in any bad behaviour).

Whatever your fall-back lesson is, just make sure you have it ready to use if and when the time comes.

Plan for Errors

07 What?! Plan for errors? That's a bit odd isn't it? I mean, can you even plan for errors? Don't they just happen?

Well, you know your subject. You know where it's easy and where it's challenging. You know the bits that cause students difficulties and the bits they usually sail through.

This means you can predict where you think errors and misconceptions are most likely to crop up. Having done so, you can plan how to deal with these – how to use them in order to make excellent teaching points.

And so planning for errors really means thinking about when and where pupils are most likely to go wrong; and then using this to help them learn how to go right.

Prompt Cards

08 These are cards which always arrive on time.

Oh dear. That was a pretty ropey joke, even by my standards.

Prompt cards are actually laminated cards you can give to pupils which provide them with prompts for reading, writing, speaking or listening. They help students to get started in activities and to keep on track when they have got going.

For example, you might create some writing prompt cards which give different ways to start a sentence. Pupils can then keep these on their desks and use them whenever they want, making the whole process of getting started on their work a lot easier.

Accept No Guessing

09 Because guessing, after all, doesn't have much to do with learning. By all means accept educated guessing, because this is underpinned by the use of reasoning (a guess becomes educated when it is based on something rather than being plucked out of thin air).

But don't accept guessing.

And don't promote it either. Ask open questions which invite reasoned responses. Use the word 'might' in your questions to indicate that many possible answers exist. And praise the processes by which pupils develop thoughtful answers, positively reinforcing the behaviour for the rest of the class.

No Hands Up

10 If you ask a question and some of your students put their hands up, what does this tell us?

A) Some students think they know the answer.

B) Some students are confident and happy to be chosen to answer.

But it doesn't tell us anything about the pupils who haven't put their hands up. Are they unconfident, disinterested or happy to sit back? Do they not know the answer or do they just see no incentive in sharing their knowledge?

Banning 'hands up' means selecting students to answer – either by design or at random. This will help you to get a more accurate sense of where everyone in the class is at, allowing you to adapt your teaching accordingly.

Answer Tokens

11 Another way to make sure you find out what a cross-section of your class are thinking and learning is by using answer tokens.

Give each pupil two or three tokens. These can be anything you like – circular discs of card or coins for example.

Every time a student answers a question they have to give in one of their tokens. This creates a system in which answers are rationed, meaning no one can dominate and increasing the likelihood that everyone will participate. Once a pupil has handed in all of their answer tokens, they are not allowed to answer a question again until you decide to redistribute the tokens.

Joker Cards

12 Joker cards create an air of surprise, shock or change which you can use in your day-to-day teaching.

Make a couple of joker cards by printing an image from the internet and then enlarging this using a photocopier before copying it onto card. One of the joker cards is for you; one is for your students.

Set a time limit in which the joker cards can be played (a week, a month or a term) and decide what you and your students will ask to happen when you play your joker cards (perhaps a completely different lesson, a favourite activity or something else).

Keep the joker cards somewhere visible in the classroom and play yours when you want (remembering that your pupils will get to do the same thing themselves).

Work the Room

13 Have you ever been to a swanky Hollywood party where the big movie star expertly works the room, talking to everybody and making them feel amazing? No, neither have I.

But the principle still applies! Working the room means interacting with people and you can work your classroom by moving around it (also known as circulating) while students are working. Ask questions, help pupils out, give praise and keep your eyes and ears open to check students' learning.

All the while you will be helping your pupils to make great progress.

Break it Down

14 Earlier on we were talking about scrap paper (see Entry Three) and how we can use this to extend the capacity of our short-term memory.

Well, another limitation we can come up against while thinking is the difficulty we have when faced with something which feels very large, perhaps even seemingly impenetrable.

Once again though, we have a method on hand to make life easier for ourselves.

Any big task becomes more manageable if we break it down. This is because we end up with lots of little tasks we can do one after the other. And, before we know it, the big task has all but vanished.

By breaking big tasks down into little tasks you will make it easier for your students to access the work and achieve success.

Activity Stations

15 This is a generic activity which you can use in any subject and with any age group. It works as follows:

Set up six or seven stations around your room. Each one should have a different activity on it connected to the topic of study. Divide the class into groups and have them move round the stations in turn, completing all the different activities.

Mix things up by using different task types, different media sources and different questions at each station.

Afterwards, have a discussion with your class where they talk to each other about the different things they did and found out.

Hand Gestures

16 Many great communicators use their body to supplement their speech. And one of the most important parts they use is their hands.

You're a great communicator – that's why you're a teacher – so, if you aren't using your hands yet, get going!

It will give your pupils another way through which to access the meaning you are trying to convey. Your hands will help students decode the words you are using, as well as the other messages you are sending out (about atmosphere, behaviour, motivation and so on).

Scanning

17 Let's set the scene for a moment. Here we are, the whole class working, getting on with the task, and you're at the front of the room wondering what to do while they work independently.

This is a perfect time for scanning.

Stay where you are and scan the room. Try to get a sense of exactly what every pupil is doing. You might scan for the big picture or you might scan for certain things such as students who need help, who are off-task or who might benefit from an extra challenge.

Scan away and then keep scanning, intermittently, so that you remain up-to-date with what's going on.

Only Share Times If They Are Definite

18 If you definitely, definitely know that an activity is going to take a certain amount of time, then by all means share this fact with your students. But only if you definitely know. Definitely.

Because if you aren't absolutely certain and you share the time with your pupils and then it turns out to be different from what you expected…

Well.

You've made yourself beholden and, if you're unlucky, the students will pick up on this and things will start going less smoothly than you had hoped.

Speak As You Mean To Go On

19 How you speak sets the standard for speech in your classroom. If you are polite then you are saying to your students that politeness is to be expected. If you speak carefully and accurately then you are sending out the message that this is the way to do things.

It doesn't mean that all pupils will automatically follow.

But it does mean that you will be modelling great speaking for them.

Which in turn means you can refer them to your own example on the occasions when they don't quite meet your expectations.

Sit Back and Let Go

20 Now, I know we all do this at the weekend, which means we have experience in the matter. So we can call on this experience when we are teaching.

Sometimes, trying to control everything, trying to remain the centre of attention, or trying to stick to a rigid schedule for the lesson can be counter-productive.

Instead, when the time feels right, sit back and let go. Let your students take the lead. Observe without intervening. Watch and listen instead of talking. Who knows, your pupils might end up surprising you.

Fast, Slow, Fast, Slow

21 Great music often varies in pace. You have a slow bit, followed by a fast bit, then maybe an extended slower period followed by a finale which gains in speed before hitting a crescendo.

This change in pace excites and interests the ear. It also helps to tell a story. The variation gives a sense of movement and direction, as if we are going somewhere rather than remaining in the same place.

It is easy to adapt the technique for your teaching. Try changing the pace in your lessons and see what happens – have fast bits followed by slow bits and so on. Play around to see the different sort of effects you can create.

Mini-Plenaries

22 Plenaries (also known as review activities or lesson wrap-ups) don't need to be confined to the end of lessons. You can use them mid-way through as well.

For example, at the end of an activity you might lead your class in a mini-plenary. This will allow you and them to quickly review the learning which has just happened.

A few benefits will accrue. First, it will help to reinforce the learning in your pupils' minds. Second, it will promote reflection and metacognition (thinking about thinking), with all the concomitant benefits this brings. Third, it will allow you to identify any misconceptions in the class as a whole.

Get Connected

23 Teaching can be lonely at times. There you are, stuck in your classroom, barely seeing another adult face all day long.

Getting connected is a good way to avoid this happening. It will also allow you to share good practice, talk about ideas and seek out help for problems.

You can connect with colleagues in your school or over the internet. Many community websites now exist, not least the best of them all: www.tes.co.uk.

Have Everything Ready

24 If you can get a lesson off to a good start you are giving yourself every chance of having a good lesson. I mean, we all know this doesn't always happen. We've all experienced that downward slide into things going wrong on at least one or two occasions, I'm sure.

Kicking off well is much better than kicking off badly though – just like in sport!

A simple approach to take involves making sure everything is ready before any students arrive. Print resources well in advance. Have your lesson saved on the computer (maybe even have a back-up on a memory stick). And, if possible, have books on desks before students sit down (so they can begin work immediately on taking their seats).

Vary Your Pitch

25 Your voice is one of the most powerful tools you have at your disposal. Varying your pitch can help you to maintain interest, gain attention and generate excitement.

If you want a good model to work from, listen to seasoned radio broadcasters or trained actors.

Tempo

26 if varying the pitch of your voice is a sound (!) technique for teaching, so too is varying the tempo at which you speak. Maybe you do this naturally already. If so, good on you.

If you don't, or if you think you could do it more effectively, try playing around with different tempos for different things you do with your voice in lessons (giving praise, explaining and giving instructions for example). See what kind of results stem from the changes your implement.

Mirroring

27 This is a body language technique which can help you to build rapport with students (and you can use it with colleagues as well if you wish).

Mirroring means unobtrusively copying the body language of the person with whom you are talking. We often do this unconsciously to signal that we agree with the speaker or to convey the message that we like them or like what they are saying.

Clearly, very obvious mirroring will not have much of an effect, other than to make pupils wonder what you are doing. Careful, understated mirroring, however, can have a big impact on your relationships with pupils and their concomitant attitudes, levels of engagement and motivation.

Build Rapport

28 While we're on the subject of building rapport, here are three further techniques you can use:

First, try weaving a little bit of humour into your lessons. People respond positively to laughter.

Second, model exemplary manners. It's very difficult not to be won over by decorum and politeness.

Third, remember pupil names and use them regularly. Everyone likes to feel that they have been remembered.

Name Recognition

29 And on that note, here's a little tip for remembering names.

When you first meet students, ask them to tell you their name and something unusual about themselves – such as a hobby, a pet they have or a holiday they have been on. As they repeat their name along with the unusual thing, really focus on pairing the two items together in your mind.

This should help to reinforce your memory of the pupils' names by creating unique links which will aid recall.

Success Criteria

30 The last few techniques have all focussed on things going on around the learning taking place in your classroom. Let's now take a different route and think about techniques closely connected to students' learning.

Our first technique is success criteria. These are the things you tell pupils they need to do in order to succeed in a task.

If you always give success criteria, your students will always have a clear sense of what they need to do to achieve. If you don't, they won't. Simple!

Task List

31 There's a lot to be said for encouraging pupils to be independent. I always feel that one of the big things is the fact that when they leave school, at whatever age that is, they are going to need to be independent whether they like it or not. Therefore, if we can help them on their way a little bit, so much the better.

An easy way to do this involves presenting your class with a list of tasks they need to complete in order to succeed in the lesson and then letting them get on with it while you help those who need help, stretch those who need to think a bit harder and generally keep an eye on things.

Checklists

32 Checklists are really a really useful tool. Many industries make use of them – medicine, manufacturing and aviation to name just three – because they allow procedures to be standardised across space and time, thus avoiding inconsistency and the potential vagaries of individual choice.

Examples of checklists you can give to pupils include:

Three things you need to do to check your work

Success criteria for a given task

Five questions to ask yourself about your writing before you hand it in

Sightlines

33 What can you see?

This is a question I'm always asking myself in the classroom. If I can't see every student, I tend to move until I can, or at least until I have been able to take in a brief visual of everybody in the room.

The reason is simple. If you don't have good sightlines and can't see all your students, how do you know who needs help, who needs an extra challenge and who's gone off task?

Process Training

34 In any lesson students make use of a variety of processes. For example: problem-solving, application of formulae, or following the instructions of a task.

Training pupils in how to successfully use or work through processes can help them to achieve success more quickly.

One technique involves taking time out from the lesson to talk to students about the process in question. You can then give pupils several opportunities to practise using or applying this process before leading a reflection in which they think and talk about how this went.

Start of Year Certificates

35 How many students get the very highest grades? It varies from class to class but, inevitably, it will never by everybody. In many cases it will be a minority of pupils when looked at overall.

Imagine, then, the kind of reaction you can get from students who have never had a top grade if you give them one. This could be the first time they have ever experienced it happening.

At the start of the year, print off and laminate a class-set of certificates. Each one should have the pupil's name written on and be signed by you. The certificate is awarded for being an 'A Grade' student. Because, after all, we want all pupils to know that is how we think of them – as an A grade person, regardless of whether they get the top grades for their work or not.

Speaking and Listening Rules

36 Speaking and listening are a central part of great teaching. For a detailed analysis of this, coupled with a wide range or practical activities and techniques, take a look at my book 'How to Use Discussion in the Classroom: The Complete Guide.'

A really easy technique you can begin using straight away is to set out clear and precise speaking and listening rules. Either develop them yourself or do it in conjunction with your class.

Police the rules, make sure pupils stick to them, model them yourself, and the benefits will soon become apparent.

Always Start With an Example

37 For example, if you are introducing a new activity, give pupils an example of how it works. Or, if you are introducing a new idea, give an example illustrating what it means or how it works.

Examples make the abstract concrete. Through this, they make things tangible, easier to understand and simpler to assimilate.

Wait-Time

38 When you ask a question…………wait.

Waiting gives students time to think. Time to think means better answers. Better answers means higher-quality teaching and learning which, in turn, means everyone in the class making more progress.

Entry Slips

39 When students are filing into your room, hand them a slip of paper with a question or task written on it. These could be the same for every pupil or a series of different ones.

Students will immediately start thinking about whatever is written on the slip and will then be able to get straight down to work upon finding their seats. As such, this is a really good way to get your lessons off to a flying start!

Scribe

40 When having a discussion with your class, appoint a scribe to make notes. These could either be on a whiteboard or on a sheet of paper. Either way, ask the student to pick out the key information which comes up during the course of the discussion.

A few nice benefits flow from this technique. First, there is a record of the discussion which everyone can see and refer to after the event. Second, the class can observe how they are developing their understanding together by looking at the various points the scribe writes down.

Starting Routines

41 The start of your lesson is a time of potential uncertainty. Students have arrived but what are they here for? How are they going to act? And what sort of mood are they in today?

You can dispel any uncertainty, neutralise problems and ensure a positive start by training your pupils in a starting routine. This way, as soon as they enter your classroom they will know exactly what is expected of them and will be in a position to get started on their work straight away.

Ending Routines

42 As with starting routines, so too with ending ones. Train your pupils so that they fall into good habits at the end of every lesson.

On a side note, you might like to throw in a joke or a bit of humour at the end of your lessons as part of the routine. This way, students leave thinking positive thoughts, reinforcing those positive connotations they already have for your lessons.

Manage Transitions

43 Transitions are those bits of the lesson where you move from one activity to the next. They can lead students to lose focus or to disengage from the learning and so it is well worth being aware of them and seeking to manage them.

To do this, try three things.

First, when planning your lessons, think about how many transitions you will have.

Second, find ways to gloss over transitions so that pupils aren't even aware that one has taken place (like when a film quickly and seamlessly switches locations).

Third, avoid moving from one complex activity to another. Insert something simple in between which provides a breathing space.

Repetition

44 It seems that sometimes repetition is frowned on in school. One line of argument says that lessons must always be fun and varied lest students lose motivation or find things boring.

Well, yes and no.

Fun and variation are good. We all know that. They create motivation, enjoyment and engagement. All of these things are good. All of them facilitate learning and progress.

But repetition and working on through boredom are also vital to success. We get better at things when we do them over and over again. Often this is neither fun nor particularly varied, but the benefits do accrue.

To prove the case, just look at any successful athlete.

Play Dumb

45 Because, if you play dumb, students will really have to work to explain their ideas to you. And this means they will be thinking harder. Which is a good thing.

Sample questions:

I don't understand. Can you explain it again?

What do you mean by that?

Go back over it again in more detail, will you?

Play Smart

46 Because this means you will be keeping students on their toes and pushing them to think more clearly and carefully about their ideas.

Sample questions:

Why do you think that?

What evidence do you have for that?

How would you explain that to an alien?

Play Helpful

47 Because playing helpful can aid students in giving birth to thoughts and ideas they may be struggling to get out.

Sample questions:

So, do you mean that...?

What made you think of that idea?

How do you think that might work in a different situation?

Play Random

48 Because playing random can help you to completely change students' perceptions, taking them to places they would never have gone otherwise, or getting them to look at the learning from a completely different angle.

Sample questions:

But what if we could disprove everything you have said so far?

How would you explain what you have just said if you could only use symbols?

What if none of the normal rules applied, what then?

Postcards

49 Postcards are nice. They usually have pretty pictures on the front. They tend to be cheap and you can pick them up from all over the place.

Put together a pack of postcards and keep them in your room. They have many uses:

Hand out a postcard to each student. Ask pupils to get into pairs and then to work out a way in which their two postcards connect.

Hand out the postcards and then challenge students to link their postcards to the learning.

Give groups a collection of postcards and ask them to use the images on the front to explain or illustrate the learning they've done during the course of the lesson.

The Evaluation Tree

50 And so here we are, number 50 of 50. The final one of our quick and brilliant teaching techniques. It's been an exciting ride but, like all journeys, it has to end somewhere. And where better than the evaluation tree?

You can get a copy at http://www.evaluationsupportscotland.org.uk/resources/227/.

It's absolutely super for getting pupils to reflect on their learning. Display the tree on your whiteboard or hand out copies of it and ask students to discuss with their partner whereabouts on the tree they think they are, in relation to the lesson or the learning.

Follow up with a whole-class discussion and then, if you like, dig the image out again in a few weeks' time and ask pupils to reflect on how they have moved up the tree in the intervening period.

A Brief Request

If you have found this book useful I would be delighted if you could leave a review on Amazon to let others know.

If you have any thoughts or comments, or if you have an idea for a new book in the series you would like me to write, please don't hesitate to get in touch at mike@mikegershon.com.

Finally, don't forget that you can download all my teaching and learning resources for **FREE** at www.mikegershon.com.

Printed in Great Britain
by Amazon.co.uk, Ltd.,
Marston Gate.